Faithbuilders Publishing

Daffodils in Winter

by Doreen Harrison

WIPF & STOCK · Eugene, Oregon

Wipf and Stock Publishers
199 W 8th Ave, Suite 3
Eugene, OR 97401

Daffodils in Winter
By Harrison, Doreen
Copyright©2019 Apostolos
ISBN 13: 978-1-5326-8088-5
Publication date 2/1/2019
Previously published by Apostolos, 2019

Cover Design by Blitz Media, Pontypool

Cover Image © Ellishaedwards | Dreamstime Stock Photos.

Other stock photo illustrations used under license from Dreamstime and are credited throughout.

With Prayer for Andrew and Sharon, and other friends who are continuing their march to Zion!

By the same author: Fragrance of Faith, A Bouquet of Blessings, A Garland of Grace, The Donkey Boy, Jubilant Jeremy Johnson, Coping with the Wobbles of Life.

Contents

This book is the latest in my series "A Bouquet of Blessings." It contains anecdotes, stories, thoughts which will hold you together when situations and circumstances are causing you to fall apart. It is a book for a bedside table, a coffee table, for a birthday gift, for a sick friend. It will fit into an A5 envelope. There are blessings in its pages, gathered through a life of variety and events which all underline the truth that Jesus saves, keeps—and satisfies—always and for ever.

Daffodils in Winter

I entered the year with confidence. Why? Well, on December 28th a local supermarket was selling British Daffodils at £1 a bunch and daffodils in December proclaim, "If winter comes, can spring be far behind?"

At a time when the media, society, and political predictions seem to emphasize doom and gloom, how we need daffodils of hope to challenge the darkness of despair! According to a recent National Trust report, that logs in painstaking detail the signs of the seasons, last year had been the year when the traditional weather boundaries blurred into one. "Haywire!" was the word the National Trust has opted to describe the weather. Who knows what this year will bring?

Well, consider the words of this old hymn, "It can bring with it nothing, but God WILL see us through. Who gives the lilies clothing, will clothe His children too. Beneath the spreading heavens, no creature but is fed, and He who feeds the ravens, will give His people bread." Maybe we are disposed to ask for cake, like Marie Antoinette? Contentment, in whatsoever state we are, is great gain.

Daffodils can be found in December! Do you remember the children's rhyme about the months of the year? "January brings the snow, makes our feet and fingers glow?" Note—they do not fall off, they glow! "February brings the rain, thaws the frozen lake again!" Let it freeze! Frozen lakes will always unfreeze!

God's promise, which has never been broken since time began, is that there will always be day after night, summer after winter, harvest to follow seedtime, and heat after cold. Daffodils can bloom in winter! How did you enter January? With trepidation? With timidity? Are you tired of trying to get life to work out for you and your family? Do you view the new year, with tears? Is it hard to trust God? In Psalm 34 there is assurance:

"I prayed to the Lord, and he answered me; he freed me from all my fears. The oppressed look to him and are glad; they will never be disappointed. The helpless call to him, and he answers; he saves them from all their troubles. His angel guards those who honor the Lord and rescues them from danger." (Psalm 34:4–7)

January

| Saturday

1~364
New Year's Day

NEW YEAR — FRESH START!

Image © Stuart Key

Happy New Year

So, it is a new year! My word, how time flies! Mark my word, the longer you live, the shorter the years seem to become! No sooner have you sung the last carol of Christmas, and wished everyone a happy new year, but it is time to begin all over again! When we offer new year greetings, we are giving a blessing for the year ahead. Those three words, "Happy New Year" when spoken sincerely, carry real potential. Words are potent! Consider these five quotations about words.

1. Words are the most powerful force available to humanity!

2. Words are like X-rays. If you use them properly, they'll go through anything. (Rudyard Kipling)

3. Words are free. It's how you use them that may cost you!

4. Value your words. Each one may be your last.

5. Of all sad words of tongue or pen, the saddest are these: It might have been. (John Greenleaf Whittier)

Time began with four words. The Bible explains, *"In the beginning, God created the heavens and the earth. … And God said, "Let there be light," and there was light."* (Genesis 1:1, 3 ESV)

The Bible explains the great celebration of Christmas like this, *"The word (Jesus) became flesh and dwelt among us, … full of grace and truth"* (John 1:14 ESV). However, when we use the words, "Happy New Year" we need to remember, with compassion, that for some people, the year ahead is already darkened with disappointment, despair, and dread concerning the unknown future. Our blessing, "Happy New Year" might sound heartless, however sincere we are.

With this in mind, I can recollect words used in the royal Christmas broadcast in 1939, when the nation was facing the darkness of World War 2 (1939–45):

> "I said to the man who stood at the gate of the year, Give me a light, that I may tread safely into the unknown. And he replied, Go out into the darkness, and put your hand into the hand of God. That shall be to you better than light and safer than a known way."

God's hands are big enough to hold all of us, safely. May every new year be a happy one for you, because your hope is in His love, His kindness and in His concern for you.

Sun After Snow

I would like to share some encouraging quotations with you:

> "In the depths of winter, I finally learned that within me there lay an invincible summer." (Albert Camus)

> "If we had no winter, the spring would not be so pleasant." (Ann Broadstreet)

> "If there were no tribulation, there would be no rest. If there were no winter, there would be no summer." (John Chrystostom)

> "April hath put a spirit of youth into everything!" (William Shakespeare)

These winsome thoughts are particularly meaningful to me, after suffering two strokes, from which, thanks to much prayer and good medical care, I am making a slow and steady recovery. First: No experience is ever wasted. Second: Every prayer is answered.

Third: There is ALWAYS light after darkness. And, yes, a winter experience makes a spring encouragement even more pleasant by contrast.

No experience is ever wasted.

When I was in the stroke unit, my grandson, a third-year medical student in Brighton, was on placement in a stroke unit there. He said, "Grandma, my approach to my work has changed: I realize now that every patient is someone's grandparent." I guess medical school could not have given him such an awareness as did my illness!

Every prayer is always answered.

One night, in hospital, I needed the toilet, and my bell wouldn't ring. What to do? Wisely, I prayed. Another elderly patient who was prone to wander, got up, wandered out of the ward, and the nurse who brought her back, saw my predicament and prayer was answered! (Albeit in a most unusual way.)

There is always light after darkness.

I am realizing yet again that nothing, absolutely nothing, can separate us from the love of God in Christ Jesus our Lord. He was with me, He will be with me, and one day, I will be with Him.

What a FRIEND we have in Jesus, all our sins and griefs to bear. What a privilege, to carry everything to God, in prayer.

Image © Tammy Venable

Find the Crocus

This is the month when crocus adorn gardens—except in ours, which is the territory of local squirrels!

Just one purple crocus has escaped their foraging. It stands in solitary splendour, in the middle of the lawn, but it proclaims, with the authority of 100 blooms, if winter comes, then spring is not far behind.

We are apt to concern ourselves with big events, special holidays, outstanding sights and sounds, but we miss out if we do not also identify the everyday pleasures each today holds. A friend of mine had a bad bout of flu and had to stay in bed. I received this delightful text from her. "You know you are loved when your daughter sends you Farley's Rusks, by Amazon, to help you get over the flu!"

I read of a third century saint, Felix of Nola, who was running from his enemies. He hid in a small cave. A busy spider spun a web over the entrance, and when his pursuers saw this, they assumed that no one had gone inside, because the web was still intact. When Felix came out, he said, "where God is, a spider's web is a wall—and where God is not, a wall is a spider's web."

Certainly, if the following quotation had been available for Saint Felix, he would have agreed, "The art of being happy does lie in the power of extracting happiness from common things."

Life is not easy, but somewhere, somehow, everyday, there will be a blessing—like the solitary crocus—if you look for it. The Bible affirms, *"This is the day that the Lord has made, let us rejoice and be glad in it."* (Psalm 118:24)

Each day is a proof that God keeps His word. He said, at the beginning of time, *"As long as the world exists, there will be a time for planting and a time for harvest. There will always be cold and heat, summer and winter, day and night"* (Genesis 8:22). Each day we can take note of the fact that God loves us, so much that He gave His only begotten son, that whoever believes in Him shall not perish, but will have everlasting life. This is not just a hope—it is a glorious fact!

Image © Ken Cole

Snow Waiting for More!

It is an undoubted fact that the dramatic snowfall we had here recently will continue in memory and conversation as long as we do. How deep, how high, how wide it was, and so unwilling to melt away!

When I was a child in Yorkshire, wise-acres would shake their heads when surveying such snowy remnants and declare, "T'snow is waiting for more snow to fetch it." Kindness characterised our society during the snowy days. Neighbours supported neighbours, drivers provided lifts, strong people wielded snow shovels on behalf of the elderly, staff willingly worked long hours and often walked long distances to ensure hospital care. Those actions will also become part of memory, but concern for each other needs to become a major feature of everyday life.

Winter provides some delightful quotations. Consider this old Japanese proverb, "One kind word can warm three winter months." An old poem I once read contained this line, "A circumstance which keeps 'till June, Decembers snow!"

We can allow cold thoughts, dark experiences, hard opinions, gripping grief, to chill our future. How can there ever be an invincible summer within me, we say. When life presents us with such steep learning curves, this thought can be a support.

If one kind word can warm three winter months, what would happen if we all began to speak peace, cheerful words, thoughtfully, forgivingly, and prayerfully to each other?

Spring always follows winter. Hope always springs eternal. Day dawns after the darkest night. The Bible advises, *"Let me hear in the morning of your steadfast love, for in you I trust. Make me know the way I should go, for to you I lift up my soul."* (Psalm 143:8 ESV)

Image © Iakov Kalinin

Frozen Milk!

One of my winsome memories of winter is the sight, sound, and smell of school milk, frozen and stacked in rows against the classroom stove to thaw out. Oh, the pleasure of the sight of those little bottles, with the top lifted off by a block of iced cream! I recall the sound as the chunk of frozen cream shrank as it melted and fell with a plop into the bottle. And then there was the homely smell of warm milk; there was powerful heat in those old stoves, which is why they were always surrounded by a high, strong barrier.

Free school milk had been around since 1906. In 1968, Harold Wilsons government withdrew free milk from secondary schools, and in 1971 Margaret Thatcher withdrew free school milk from children under 7—a policy which earned her the nickname, "Thatcher, the milk snatcher!"

I used the adjective winsome to describe the pleasant memory of those small glass bottles with shiny silver tops; for time can snatch away the content of an event, but not the memory.

Winsome means something which is generally pleasing and engaging, often because of a childlike charm and innocence. The word began a 1000 years ago, and was formed from the old English word *wynn*, which means pleasure. It became win, but that noun has changed its meaning somewhat since the 17th century. As time marches on, it seems that we lose some and win some. Would a class of children now have "win" if presented with a small bottle of lukewarm milk at break time?

Certainly, the provision of milk represented daily concern for the overall wellbeing of the nation's children. Nowadays standards of living in the UK are high. Free school milk would perhaps be a luxury rather than a necessity. However, each of us is a trinity of body, mind, and spirit. We care well for body and mind, but what about our spiritual development? I used to drink my daily quota of milk against a wall which was decorated with the Lord's prayer, painted in beautiful script. Body, mind, and spirit! Every day included sincere prayer to open school and to close school.

Consider these words from the Bible, *"You created me, and you keep me safe; give me understanding, so that I may learn your laws"* (Psalm 119:73). We must make sure that time and progress do not snatch away an awareness of Gods law. We must always require that children are nourished spiritually, for this is a necessity, not a luxury.

The Quiet of Easter

Why was it so quiet that first Easter morning? We would have expected the heavenly host to be there, singing "Alleluia!" as Jesus Christ strode out of his death cave, alive for ever more. But there was just one angel, sitting nonchalantly on the stone he had rolled away—no trumpets, no obvious triumph, just the clearness of early dawn, the sweet song of the birds, and the faithful women, who came to mourn the dead.

Why so low key? Why? Because God always wins. He is infallible, ineffable, inexpressibly accurate in everything He does, and because He is so great and glorious we must always expect amazing acts of grace and not be amazed when His miracles are presented to us.

Of course, Jesus came back from the dead! He is God, Saviour, Prince of Peace. We can depend on Him to be with us now and throughout all eternity. He is the mighty conqueror.

The quiet loveliness of the early morning in the garden underlines the fact that, *"For God loved the world so much that he gave his only Son, so that everyone who believes in him may not die but have eternal life"* (John 3:16). This glorious truth needs no decoration to improve its wonderful impact on time and eternity. The scene in the garden is a declaration of Jesus promise, *"Peace is what I leave with you; it is my own peace that I give you. I do not give it as the world does. Do not be worried and upset; do not be afraid."* (John 14:27)

One day, at the name of Jesus, every knee will bow, in heaven and on earth, and under the earth, and every tongue will acknowledge Jesus Christ is Lord, to the glory of God the father (see Philippians 2:10–11). Then the heavenly host will sing—then the sky will thrill with rapture—but on the first Easter morning, bird song was sufficient acclaim for the undeniable fact that Christ IS risen, He is risen indeed.

Image © David Hubbard

Alive Forever!

So, another Easter has finished? Actually, Easter never ends! Consider again the events of that first Easter. Very early in the morning, some women came to the tomb where Jesus body had been laid.

A heavy stone sealed the entrance—but now the stone had been rolled away, and the body had gone! Two angels, dressed in white clothes that gleamed like lightening, were sitting inside the cave, one at the head and the other at the foot of the slab on which the body had been laid, and the grave cloths—strips of linen—were neatly folded between them. The angels made the announcement, "He is not here. He is risen!"

But it was a very low-key way in which to announce such a stupendous event! Surely it deserved the return of that multitude of the heavenly host, praising God, as they had done 33 years before when Jesus was born in Bethlehem? Here there were just two angels, giving the tremendous news to a small group of women.

And where would they find Jesus? An angel told them, *"He has been raised from death, and now he is going to Galilee ahead of you; there you will see him"* (Matt 28:7). In Galilee? Why not in Jerusalem, gloriously triumphant in His temple there? Why not blazing with his risen presence before Pilate, thus providing a vivid, vital, vibrant answer to Pilates question, "Are you the King of the Jews?" Why such a quiet presentation of the incredible truth that Jesus, Messiah, is alive for ever more—and you can't kill God.

The simple fact is that God doesn't need to make a flamboyant display. Jesus is the Way, the Truth, and the Life. God presented Jesus to be the Saviour of the world, and when Jesus fulfilled that purpose and was crucified, dead, and buried, of course He rose again, just as He said He would. The powerful words spoken by the angel are these, *"He is going before you into Galilee. You will see Him there."* Jesus spent the days before he ascended into heaven with his friends, in Galilee, meeting them in the ordinary affairs of daily life.

This is the abiding message of Easter! Jesus is with us, always. He has promised, *"I will never leave you; I will never abandon you."* (Hebrews 13:5)

Indeed, Easter is for ever!

The Street Sweeper

Here is an old story which contains a lot of wisdom. "For want of a nail, the shoe was lost. For want of a shoe, the horse was lost. For want of a horse, the rider was lost. For want of a rider, the battle was lost. For want of the battle, the kingdom was lost! And all for the want of a horse shoe nail."

Society is so impressed by big names, great performances, by large crowds, and prestigious events. But in this story, we have one workman, one hammer, one missing nail affecting the entire future of the kingdom and everyone in it. It is an amazing fact that an individual can be accountable for events which affect the majority. Martin Luther put it like this, "If a man is called to be a street sweeper, he should sweep streets even as Michelangelo painted, or Beethoven composed music, or Shakespeare wrote poetry. He should sweep streets so well, that all the hosts of heaven and earth will pause to say, Here is a great street sweeper, who did his job well."

Consider the account of David the Shepherd boy, defeating the giant Goliath. The Bible reads like this, *"Goliath started walking toward David again, and David ran quickly toward the Philistine battle line to fight him. He reached into his bag and took out a stone, which he slung at Goliath. It hit him on the forehead and broke his skull, and Goliath fell face downward on the ground. And so, without a sword, David defeated and killed Goliath with a sling and a stone!"* (1 Samuel 17:48–50)

David worked well, with what he had—his own tools. But he also declared, *"I come in the name of the Lord God Almighty,"* (1 Samuel 17:45) which is why he won the battle. A thought for parents, pupils, and teachers at the beginning of the new school year. Parents encourage your children to work well. Pupils work well. Only one person can be top of the class—it might not be your position but work well with your own abilities. Teachers enjoy your work. A Lecturer at my college said, "Always remember—the future Prime Minister might be in your class!" Prime minister—Michelangelo—Beethoven—street sweeper—who ever, whatever, work well! And may God bless us all.

Image © Foodio

Come and Celebrate!

Every breakfast is a celebration meal. We understand that this is especially true of a wedding breakfast—a new beginning—but in fact *every breakfast* signals the beginning of a new day, and that gift of another 24 hours of life, deserves celebration. Yesterday is past, tomorrow has yet to come, but today is yours.

The most unusual breakfast I ever had was in an African village, on the equator. Bread was newly baked, and we waited for the rest of the meal. We had a long wait. Our host explained, "we cannot give you food until the chickens have laid the eggs for you." On the other extreme, the most opulent breakfast I attended was a banquet breakfast in the USA, where 500 guests had gathered to hear me, the English speaker!

Succulent course followed succulent course. When I finally stood up to greet them, I was amazed that anyone was still awake. My most emotional breakfast followed my father's death, in hospital.

We were at his bedside as dawn broke and he took his last breath. We went to break the news to his mother. Tears rolled down her face and then she said, "But this is a new day, and we will have breakfast together."

The three breakfasts I have described all have one thing in common. Firstly, there was waiting time. We waited for the chickens to lay the eggs. We waited until every item on the long breakfast menu had been served and enjoyed. We waited, through a long night, and then waited with family, as the sad news was unfolded. Now, consider these words from the Bible. *"The steadfast love of the Lord never ceases; his mercies never come to an end; they are new every morning; great is your faithfulness. 'The Lord is my portion,' says my soul, 'therefore I will hope in him.'"* (Lamentations 3:22–26)

The promise given to Noah has never been broken. God promises, *"As long as the world exists, there will be a time for planting and a time for harvest. There will always be cold and heat, summer and winter, day and night"* (Genesis 8:22). Notice the order here: day, then night, then day. Even the darkest night of discontent, discomfort, distress, or despair is sandwiched between day and day. Consider again, *"The Lord's unfailing love and mercy still continue, Fresh as the morning, as sure as the sunrise."* (Lamentations 3:22–23)

As the song writer put it, "Morning has broken, like the first morning, Blackbird has spoken, like the first bird. Praise for the singing, praise for the morning, praise for them springing, fresh from the word." Nothing can separate us from the love of God in Christ Jesus our Lord.

Red Sky at Night

Dust snatched from the Sahara, and wild fires in Portugal, combined to turn British skies red, until the sunlight broke through and carried the dust and smoke away. The light was not overcome by the darkness, nor was it extinguished.

I remember certain evenings in the Congo, Africa, when the light presented with a quality that was quite theatrical, and which local people called, "The light of the leopard." The unusual quality of that light made it difficult for the leopard to hunt, unseen by its prey. Light reveals danger and promotes safety.

A friend sent me an account of a holiday in Alaska. She wrote, "The flowers in Alaska are huge! Even the dandelions are standing 2 feet above the grass and their blooms are 6 inches across." Why are the flowers so big? Because in summer, there is almost 20 hours of sunshine! Such is the potential of light.

Light is silent, but its presence speaks louder than words. Creating light was the first act of creation. The Bible explains, *"The earth was formless and desolate. The raging ocean that covered everything was engulfed in total darkness, and the Spirit of God was moving over the water. Then God commanded, "Let there be light"—and light appeared"* (Genesis 1:2–3). Someone told me that the most frightening words they ever heard were during the 1939–45 war, when an Air Raid Warden in the street outside her home said, "Put that light out!" When they did, it was completely dark. Today we face spiritual enemies: doubt, despair, distrust, dismay, difficult decisions, double dealing, debt, disease discontent, dark thoughts, deep loneliness, and disbelief. Without the light of the knowledge of the glory of God in the face of Jesus Christ, fear might overwhelm us. BUT God's light is inextinguishable!

A prayer which always prevails uses these words, "Lighten our darkness, we beseech Thee, o Lord, and by Thy great mercy, defend us from all perils and dangers of this night." Amen to that.

Image © Hladkymartin

Mountains of Safety

As I read a newspaper article titled, "Go on a walk and pick up rubbish!" I thought of a recent E Mail, from my granddaughter who is using part of her gap year to work with Tear Fund in Cambodia. She writes:

> We were involved in a clean the streets parade, where we marched alongside the Mayor all the way through Poipet. We had one day to come up with a dance routine with some brooms and then 30 minutes to teach some high school kids the dance routine! We marched along, cleaning up the city, the Mayor in his crisp white shirt and fancy shoes getting stuck in, as a representation to the whole city that we should look after it. An amazing opportunity for the church to get involved as well!

At this point, my attention is drawn to another article in a local newspaper concerning a Baptist church. I quote, "The church will be the meeting point for the monthly Community Litter Pick. Cleaning up the area will be followed by free tea\coffee and biscuits."

We are all involved in keeping the area where we live clean, friendly, and litter free. It is so easy to look at litter and leave it! Maybe we all need to become active and pick it up. And, of course, you never know what you might find in the process! Consider this story.

A man had travelled 1000 miles across the US To attend his mother's funeral. As he waited in the bus station for the bus which would take him home, he was cold and weary with grief. The bus arrived. He looked in his wallet for his ticket. It wasn't there. He searched his pockets. No ticket. There was a litter of paper tissue, rubbish around his feet. He picked it up and, yes, there was the missing ticket! Picking up litter is a personal and productive activity—do we really need persuasion to make it a predictable activity? However, there would be no litter to pick up if we did not drop litter in the first place!

With this in mind, remember the advice in the Bible, *"love your neighbour as you love yourself"* (Mark 12:31). We share our own space—with everyone else.

Image © Stuart Key

Recycling Headache

The issue of large dustbins with purple lids, brown bins for kitchen waste, green bins for garden rubbish, and black boxes for recyclable items, has become an acceptable asset to life here in Torfaen. The other day, I had an unusual encounter with the convenience of the system. I took a small bag of food waste, opened the large bin by mistake, and dropped it in! As I leaned over to retrieve it, the bin slipped, so did I! I was faced with two choices. Fall into the bin (I am a small lady) or let the bin fall on me!

What did I do? I PRAYED. Then, almost gracefully, I slid to the ground. The bin missed me, but a large plastic bag, full of soft rubbish slid under my head, like a pillow. And I fell into a puddle, full of soft mud, rather than onto the hard concrete! I struggled to my feet, and I have never appreciated the cleansing comfort of a hot shower as much as I did then. There are lessons to learn from my mishap:

1.   Keep your mind on what you are doing. I opened the wrong bin because I wasn't concentrating on the job in hand.

2.   Look for the best in any situation, rather than the worst. Consider the soft plastic bag, like a pillow, because sharp, smelly, cutting, bruising rubbish was in other containers! And our regular rain, which had covered the hard concrete with a protective puddle of mud. Remember the old adage and identify your circumstances as like a glass half full, not half empty.

3.   Pray, without ceasing. Our God is a very present help in time of trouble. The Bible reminds us, *"Do not be afraid—I am with you! I am your God—let nothing terrify you! I will make you strong and help you; I will protect you and save you."* (Isaiah 41:10)

4.   Be grateful for all the benefits of the society in which we live—even for the regularity of our rubbish collections! Many people live in places where there is fear, famine, wide spread poverty, and streets in which rubbish piles up, because there is no political stability, and where prayer to our God is classified as a suspect activity. But keep in mind another Bible verse, *"Work for the good of the cities where I have made you go as prisoners. Pray to me on their behalf, because if they are prosperous, you will be prosperous too."* (Jeremiah 29:7)

Circumstances can change. Only God is unchanging. Find out the goodness of the Lord for yourself! Ministry is available for you at your local church—why not go along and see?

Image © Thomas Schmitt

Remember Jesus

I recollect a story about a man who had a greyhound—and that dog was a winner! It was like a mobile xylophone, lean, with every rib visible. He trained it so well that whenever it was entered in a race, it won. It was the Bookies nightmare-dog, but the punters delight. And then, one evening, this amazing dog actually caught the rabbit!

Things changed after that. No longer was the dog certain to win. He became a slow starter. Sometimes he even stopped running in the middle of the race and sauntered to the side of the track to allow the other dogs to rush past! Finally, his owner withdrew him from the lists and the dog became a household pet. Those ribs were hidden under his glossy coat. "What happened?" inquired a relieved Bookie. His owner replied, "He just gave up the chase when he discovered that the rabbit wasn't real." He became a happy dog, instead of a hunter for achievement.

There is a moral in this story. People run after ambition, promotion at work, luck in the lottery, success in society, but—like the rabbit—none of these really satisfy. We compete with all our energy, our intention is to succeed at all costs, and yet, unfortunately, and unfailingly, we end up with the realisation that we have been chasing rabbits which are not real. At which point, we can stop trying, lose heart, or with dogged determination we can begin to identify what are life's real values, and enjoy the situations which suit us best—and, maybe, let the other dogs win.

The Bible advises, *"Trust in the Lord with all your heart. Never rely on what you think you know. Remember the Lord in everything you do, and he will show you the right way. Never let yourself think that you are wiser than you are; simply obey the Lord and refuse to do wrong. If you do, it will be like good medicine, healing your wounds and easing your pains."* (Proverbs 3:5–8)

The statement, "you can't take it with you when you die!" is so true. Position, power, possessions, poverty, pain, whatever we have, whoever we are, however we have lived, one day life's race ends. The reality then is how we are related to God, through faith in Jesus Christ. When He is real to us, then, indeed His goodness and mercy will dog our path to its earthly conclusion: and we will, *"dwell in the house of the Lord for ever."* (Psalm 23:6 ESV)

Image © Kapsandui Andrew

Be Thankful

Summer continues to live up to its reputation as the season of hot sunshine, blue skies, Wimbledon tennis, cricket, sports day at school and holidays! Here in the UK we can enjoy all these things, because we live in the affluent West. It is dangerously easy to take all these things for granted, or even to assume that we have a right to have work wages, good food, peace on our streets, and pensions when we retire.

Situations can change! We must be grateful for what we have now, while we have all these benefits. Maybe the grace which is usually said before meals, "For what we are about to receive, may the Lord make us truly thankful," should be used as an introduction to each day; and its partner, "For what we HAVE received, may the Lord make us truly thankful," should be our epitaph at the end of each day.

In one of my classes were some immigrant children. One day, Sarbjit greeted me with excitement. "We've got a new shower! Come and see it after school. Mum says you can!"

I went home with Sarbjit. The family proudly showed me the shower. It was in a shed, outside the back door, with the shower head fixed to the wooden roof, cold water only, but luxury for a family whose original home had no water supply and no back door! I came away, honoured to have met such truly grateful people.

In Northern Uganda, there is a refugee camp that is "home" (!) to 300,000 people and aptly named Bidi Bidi, which means "multitude." One of the refugees said, "Trauma is the biggest problem in this camp. We experience a great struggle just to keep alive." The children in Bidi Bidi are constantly afraid.

I do not tell you these things to cast a cloud over our lovely summer here in the UK. I do want us all, myself included, to remember that, "There, but for the grace of God, go I." The Bible reminds us:

> "Praise the Lord, my soul! All my being praise his holy name! Praise the Lord, my soul, and do not forget how kind he is."
> (Psalm 103:1–2)

Image © Sokkete

Beautiful Sounds

With the royal wedding date fixed, I noted a new anxiety concerning its presentation in the media. Because Windsor Castle is under a flight path to Heathrow Airport, they worried over how they were to tune out the noise of the aircraft! Noise! It permeates every aspect of modern society. Even triple glazed windows are insufficient to combat the trauma and turbulence of traffic on ordinary roads, let alone under a flight path, or near a motorway!

The other day, however, I encountered noise with a difference. Walking around a local reservoir, the noise of twanging masts on moored boats, beside the yacht club, the different notes of sheep and lambs bleating in harmony, the gurgle, plunge and splash of waves, birds in the trees and childrens voices in the distance—all united together to present a veritable symphony of spring! Maybe the next time I encounter noise, with annoyance, I should realise, with gratitude, that I can hear the noise.

Maybe we take for granted our sense of hearing—until we begin to lose it! Recently, a violinist sued the Royal Opera House in London for damaging his hearing during rehearsals for Wagner's Ring cycle. The sound peaked at 137 decibels, around the level of a jet engine. He was awarded damages of thousands of pounds. Thus, justice attempted to put a price on the ability to hear easily and clearly. Of course, it does matter what we hear. A continual avalanche of distress, despair, disobedience, debt, dismay, discord will make everybody reach for ear muffs! I am always impressed by the account in the Bible, describing how Jesus heals a deaf man, *"So Jesus took him off alone, away from the crowd, put his fingers in the man's ears, spat, and touched the man's tongue. Then Jesus looked up to heaven, gave a deep groan, and said to the man, 'Ephphatha,' which means, 'Open up!'"* (Mark 7:33–34)

Jesus gave the man privacy from the clamouring crowd, he acted out the healing—looking up to heaven, sighing to show his concern, pulling out the deafness from his ears! He treated this man with respect, with courtesy, with kindness. Now—how do we react to deaf people? How does our Council, our schools, society as a whole, meet the needs of this important part of our community?

Image © Srlee2

Music of the Lake

We were sitting by a lake, which was sustained by several streams, and enhanced by a central fountain. The water lilies were in full bloom, the sky was blue, and I became aware of the music! There were deep notes where one of the streams entered the lake over a series of little waterfalls. There were tinkling chords as the water lapped against stones on the bank. There was a crescendo of splashes as the fountain spray rose and fell. From all sides, different sounds combined to make water music that exalted the beauty of a summer day in Wales. I was hearing a symphony – and if just one watery note had been missing the entire effect would have been limited.

I remember reading about an orchestral performance at which the conductor suddenly stopped the orchestra. Consternation. What was wrong? He explained, "I couldn't hear the piccolo." Now, if the drum—or the trumpet—or the large cymbal—had fallen silent, his action might have seemed credible! But the thin piping note of a piccolo!? The conductor continued, "For complete harmony, every instrument is important. So, piccolo, please – play your part."

In the orchestra of life, everyone is important. This is an amazing statement when we consider that records show that over 7.5 BILLION people populate planet earth! More than three million of them live in Wales.

The Bible affirms, *"For only a penny you can buy two sparrows, yet not one sparrow falls to the ground without your Father's consent. As for you, even the hairs of your head have all been counted. So do not be afraid; you are worth much more than many sparrows!"* (Matthew 10:29–31)

Incredible as it may seem, our faith asserts that each person who is, or was, or will be a citizen on Earth is known to God! We are all included in the great chorus of Creation. The music of our living is important. So – how tuneful are we? Do we keep our attention on the Conductor? Do we check the score (the Bible)? Or have we stopped playing His melody?

Image © Martinmark

Ice Cream Shortage

The headline declared, "Stock up the freezer, vanilla ice cream is in short supply!" Vanilla. It is the only fruit bearing member of the orchid family, with flowers that only last for one day. Then the bean is picked, dried, and cured in a process that can take up to 6 months.

85 per cent of all vanilla comes from Madagascar, where recent weather conditions have devastated the crop, meaning that vanilla has become the world's most expensive spice, costing more than silver!

A news item showed anxious ice cream manufacturers discussing how they could produce ice cream, using vanilla for flavouring, at a price which the licking public would be willing to pay. Of course, there are ways of producing artificial vanilla flavouring using various unappetising ingredients, including wood and even petrol!

Just after the war, ice cream was produced using potatoes! It did not hit the headlines!

On reflection, it was reassuring to see and hear a headline about vanilla. Amongst media reports of shootings, murder, betrayal, nuclear weapons, the cost of living, LED lighting as a possible cause of cancer (!), a discussion concerning the flavour of vanilla ice cream in the future was quite a relief!

A modern approach to stress relief is "mindfulness." This guides us to focus attention on the present, on what is happening here and now, to stay in the moment. I pick up a phrase from the description of vanilla: The flower lasts only one day. The Bible declares, *"This is the day that the Lord has made; let us rejoice and be glad in it."* (Psalm 118:24 ESV)

Jesus advises, *"Therefore do not be anxious about tomorrow, for tomorrow will be anxious for itself. Sufficient for the day is its own trouble."* (Matthew 6:34 ESV)

Saint Paul's declaration, *"I have learned to be satisfied with what I have"* (Philippians 4:11) is undoubtedly the right ambition for a fragrant, fruitful and faith filled life.

Vanilla is more expensive than silver—but consider this verse:

"knowing that you were ransomed … not with perishable things such as silver or gold, but with the precious blood of Christ, like that of a lamb without blemish or spot." (1 Peter 1:18–19 ESV)

Faith cannot be valued in human terms. Be mindful of this!

Trust His Word

Consider these words from Proverbs, *"Trust in the Lord with all your heart, and do not lean on your own understanding. In all your ways acknowledge him, and he will make straight your paths. Be not wise in your own eyes; fear the Lord, and turn away from evil."* (Proverbs 3:5–7 ESV)

I praise the Lord for the accuracy of His word. On a recent Saturday night, we were in the centre of the city of Bristol. Saturday night in Bristol is certainly NOT like it is in the South Wales valleys! The area abounds with restaurants and clubs, and the streets were full of young people, out for a good time. We did not match the crowds. In fact, the security guards outside one of the clubs made a point of saluting us, maybe to reassure us of their presence? Obviously, there was no place to park our car! So we prayed for guidance. Then, we saw a space, outside one of the clubs. We prayed again, parked the car and trusted God's wisdom, not our own. When we returned, the car was still there, in splendid isolation, although I really expected to see angels, keeping guard over it!

I do not advocate parking outside a busy night club in the centre of a city on a Saturday night. BUT I do emphasise the fact of faith, that when you trust in God, He never lets you down. Proverbs 3 also contains these words, *"My son, do not forget my teaching, but let your heart keep my commandments, for length of days and years of life and peace they will add to you."* (Proverbs 3:1–2 ESV)

Do we store God's promises in our memory bank? Do we hold His truths there, ready to draw on when we need them? It would be wise for all of us to learn God's word, to build up a supply of His advice and wisdom. Psalm 119 verse 11 states, *"I keep your law in my heart, so that I will not sin against you."* Verse 14 continues, *"I delight in following your commands more than in having great wealth."*

How about this for a handy Bible couplet?

A verse a day keeps the devil away!

Image © Darius Strazdas

Saved by a Spider

These long, lazy days of summer, and the school holidays, are an ideal opportunity to build family relationships and to create memories which will enhance many a family occasion in future years! We often remember when we took our granddaughter Lotte to Bristol Zoo. We saw the elephant, gigantic giraffes, mobile monkeys, penguins, all sorts and conditions of bird, beast, and water creatures. When we asked, "What did you like the best?" she replied, "That little spider web, sparkling like diamonds!" Beside one of the pathways, woven between tall fronds of grass, was a tiny web, spangled with raindrops which reflected the sunshine; and it was very beautiful.

Maybe this early experience explains why Lotte doesn't suffer from arachnophobia. Of course, the problem with spiders is that the direction in which they will make their next move is unpredictable, probably because 8 legs offer variety of direction and also maximise speed!

There is a delightful legend concerning a spider. When King Herod's soldiers were pursuing Joseph, Mary and Jesus, the holy family hid in a cave. A spider spun a web over the cave entrance. When soldiers reached the cave, the officer in command said, "Keep moving! Look at that spider web. No one has gone in there recently."

Saved – by a spider!

The legend may not be true, but it is indeed true that, *"We know that in all things God works for good with those who love him, those whom he has called according to his purpose"* (Romans 8:28). Also, consider these words from Isaiah, chapter 41, verse 10, *"Do not be afraid—I am with you! I am your God—let nothing terrify you! I will make you strong and help you; I will protect you and save you."*

God, your Father, understands how, when and why you are afraid, and when you come to Him for help—fear scuttles away (just like a spider)!

Taking the Test

Exams are over, results will decide what happens next. However, determined people succeed without the decision of exam results! If I had to select one person who succeeded against all odds, it would be a small woman named Gladys Aylward, who was born in London over 100 years ago.

Gladys was a parlour maid, because she wasn't clever enough to do anything else! But Gladys was a Christian. She believed that God wanted her to be a missionary in China. She enrolled in a Bible Training college, but soon into the course, the Principal told her that she really wasn't up to the standard required and advised her to go back into service.

At this news, Gladys determined to take herself to China. She worked extra hours, she saved, she prayed, and, eventually, she reached China. She became an Inn keeper, in a remote town, in the North, providing accommodation for Mule trains. Each evening, when muleteers and animals had been fed, she told them stories about God and His love for humankind. Thus, she provided food, shelter, entertainment.

One morning, as she was clearing up after the night before, an anxious messenger arrived from the Prison. "Come. You must come at once. There is a riot! You must come, and stop it!" He insisted, pleaded, and at last, a reluctant Gladys went with him.

There was certainly a riot! The shouts and screams echoed over the prison wall. The Governor was waiting outside the large prison gate, "You have come! Only you can stop them killing each other!" Gladys looked at him in amazement. She said, "I can't stop them. If I go in there, they'll kill me as well." "How can they kill you?" replied the Governor. "You say that you carry the Living God in your heart. How can they kill God?" Gladys realised that He was speaking the truth. "Let me in!" she said. He unlocked the big gate and locked it behind her. The prison yard was full of fighting men. There were dead bodies, pools of blood. Gladys took a deep breath. She remembered the Bible promise, *"I can do all things through him who strengthens me"* (Philippians 4:13). She shouted above the noise, "STOP IT AT ONCE!" And they did! That small woman regained control

Now, how did Gladys succeed against all the odds? Certainly not through her own ability! She had a determined faith to trust God what ever happened. The Bible has sound advice, *"Trust in the Lord with all your heart, and do not lean on your own understanding"* (Proverbs 3:5). God will NEVER let you down.

Image © Ikonoklastfotographie

Cashing Up

Having finished school, what next? For some teenagers, there is a gap between comprehensive school and college/ university, and they look for paid work, to provide for various activities, and to augment the cost of further education. For others, there will be a search for full time employment and provision for the next stage in life.

My first job was as a Saturday girl in Woolworths. Although Woolworths was in the main shopping street, it was an old-fashioned establishment. Each department had its own square of counters, and the assistant in charge was inside this box like structure. I was invariably in "Do-it-yourself!" Nuts and bolts, screws, nails, tools. I was seldom inundated with customers, and those who did come, knew exactly what they wanted and showed me where to find them. In those days, nails were sold by weight, "Half a pound of 6-inch nails, please!" I got a wage packet at the end of the day, and I learned to appreciate the discipline and dignity of work. At closing time, the manager would stand where he could see all the assistants, and at his command, we would "ding!" open our cash registers, and the cashier would collect the days takings. Thus, I learned that I was responsible for my little part in earning money for big Woolworths. I was accountable for what was in my cash register. I learned that work requires honesty discipline and identifies us with the dignity of contributing to the welfare of society.

In my Woolworth overall, amongst the mysterious "Do-it-yourself" conglomeration, I was only aware that a wage packet awaited me. Later I appreciated the value of that first job.

In the story of Creation, the first people, Adam and Eve, were given the responsibility of work. The Bible states, *"Then the Lord God placed the man in the Garden of Eden to cultivate it and guard it"* (Genesis 2:15). When God sent Jesus to be the Saviour of the world, He placed him in a family in Nazareth, and his first work was as a carpenter. It is important that our young people are not denied the advantage of learning the discipline and dignity of working for their living. Providing many opportunities for work, for apprenticeships, should feature large in the policy of any government. The Bible advises, *"Train up a child in the way he should go; even when he is old he will not depart from it."* (Proverbs 22:6 ESV)

Image © Inara Prusakova

Starting School

I remember him well. Joe was a dwarf. For 7 years his embarrassed parents had excluded him from the village. He had never played in the garden, been seen in the local general store, certainly never started school. When I began a teaching position there, and realised the situation, I made an early opportunity to call at his home. Eventually it was agreed that Joe could begin school. I prepared the other children. "Joe is coming to school" I said. "His outside is different, but inside he is just like you. And it is the inside which is important."

Joe settled in well. He was cheerful, cooperative, and in the 18 months I was there, he began to learn and catch up with his peers. Many years later, I revisited the village, and I met up with Joe. I could still pat him on the head, but Joe had done well. He had a job in the local water works, he drove his own small car, he had been provided with a bungalow. He gave me the biggest compliment I have ever had. He said, "Miss, you encouraged me to have confidence in myself." That is the accolade every teacher works for, that each pupil feels self-confident.

These days school success is coded through colour bandings, from red, the worst, to green, the best. A report on local schools informs us that, "The majority of local schools are achieving green ranking." That's great for the greens, but what about the reds? I discovered that 5 local schools are in the red band. However, the person responsible for education in our county assures us, "We will give the right support to schools in the red band when and where they need it, in a timely and targeted way."

We must encourage our local schools, teachers, governors, staff, pupils. Do not let our hopes be dwarfed by what was. Aim high for what might be achieved. Most of all, pray for our schools. God is even more concerned than we are, and He always hears and answers prayers! Consider these words from the Bible, *"The Lord watches over those who obey him, those who trust in his constant love."* (Psalm 33:18)

Image © Andrew Chittock

Tragedy or Victory?

We visited the Welsh Guards museum in Brecon, where there is an amazing collection of regimental artefacts and mementoes. Our visit was enhanced by the presence of an ex-Guardsman with 30 years of service, who regaled us with stories of the army and anecdotes from its past history. There is one room full of rifles, another full of medals, a large model of the strategy of the battle of Rourke's Drift, a plethora of military uniforms and equipment. But the object which really took my attention was—a teddy bear!

Pocket size, weather worn, battered, the label informed that it had been found lying in the mud, in a trench, in the 1914–18 war and rescued. Its owner was presumed dead. This was such a poignant reminder of the futility of war! I imagined a young man, maybe only just 17 years old, leaving his village with splendid intentions, but carrying this little bear as a comforting reminder of home and security. Perhaps it was a superstitious emblem of hope, but it was surely a constant reminder of friends, family, and future when the war was over. I was grateful that someone rescued little Teddy and brought it home!

Of course, we have to fight for what is right, to eradicate what is wrong. Recent battles provoke anger, because it seems that civilians have been used as human shields. But any warfare in the 21st century can deliver absolute mayhem such is the indiscriminate power of modern weaponry. Politicians proclaim that if the nuclear key was turned, no one would win. The whole world would be involved in nuclear fall-out and time would be no more. Such is my reaction to that little Teddy bear, a treasure of hope, rescued from the past.

Consider, then, this advice from the Bible, *"I urge that petitions, prayers, requests, and thanksgivings be offered to God for all people; for kings and all others who are in authority, that we may live a quiet and peaceful life with all reverence toward God and with proper conduct. This is good and it pleases God our Savior"* (1 Timothy 2:1–3). What we pray now, in the present, will certainly affect the future. Please take your responsibility in elections seriously. Pray for wisdom as you cast your vote. Pray for each candidate, for every member of the next government, and pray for all leaders of all nations. Entreat God for peace in our time. Take time, in prayer to trust God to turn the hearts of all humanity towards Him, with hope.

Then, Teddy's unknown owner might not have died in vain!

THEIR NAME LIVETH
FOR EVERMORE

Image © Havana1234

Remember

We will remember them! This verbal declaration is universally made on 11th November—but why do we remember, and how? Parades, poppies, hopes that the ferocity of war will never again overwhelm our nation, and fears that such a hope is, really, hopeless. How do we react to the tradition of the 11th hour of the 11th day of the 11th month, when we take 2 minutes of silence to celebrate peace on earth? Or does this particular declaration of peace and goodwill to all men belong to the 25th day of the 12th month? There is poignant carol with these words, "O hush your noise, ye men of strife, and hear the angels sing." We need to partner these words with the social promise, "We will remember them!" The mud, the squalor, the stench of the trenches demonstrated the complete futility of that 1914—18 war. The instant annihilation presented by the hydrogen bomb in the 1939—45 war declared the irresponsibility of human warfare. A third world war could possibly result in absolute silence in which time would be no more.

It is vital that the social calendar makes space to remember. A 2-minute silence is a token, but it matters that we observe the tradition. Prayer is no longer on the agenda of our national life, or so it would seem, but 2 minutes, when we "hush the noise," is a type of prayer, a national repentance for what was, what is, and what might be, unless God intervenes.

The Bible offers this advice, *"First of all, then, I urge that petitions, prayers, requests, and thanksgivings be offered to God for all people; for kings and all others who are in authority, that we may live a quiet and peaceful life with all reverence toward God and with proper conduct. This is good and it pleases God our Savior, who wants everyone to be saved and to come to know the truth."* (1 Timothy 2:1–4)

In many Remembrance parades and services, this old hymn will be sung, "O God, our help in ages past, our hope for years to come, our shelter from the stormy blast – and our eternal home."

As you wear your poppy, pray that the fields of despair will brighten with flowers of faith and hope. We expect a bright tomorrow! All will be well.

Image © Eugene Bochkarev

Christmas Dinner

Christmas dinner is often described as, "the meal of the year." Christmas food is traditional and for centuries we have feasted on turkey, Christmas pudding, and mince pies—with a break of a few years, when Cromwell declared that Christmas requires fasting, not feasting, and these foods were banned!

Turkey came to UK tables in 1526. King Henry 8th is recorded as having eaten it with enthusiasm at Christmas, although his size would indicate that he always enjoyed his food.! This year it is estimated that 10 million turkeys will be roasted and relished!

In the 14th century, a porridge called Frumenty, made from beef, mutton, raisins, currants, spices, and prunes, was served on Christmas Eve. In the 1950s it was still traditional food in some farming communities. The recipe changed, in content and shape, but frumenty is the origin of Christmas pudding. Mince pies were introduced in the 13th century. Crusaders brought the recipe back from their war in the Middle East. The recipe included minced meat, flavoured with alcohol, fruit and spices, to preserve the meat.

Other names were Shrid pies, Crib pies—shaped like a cradle, to remind the eater that Jesus was born at Christmas, and Wayfarers pies, because they were offered to visitors and travellers at Christmas. An old tradition stated that the year ahead would be a good year if you ate a mince pie on each of the 12 days of Christmas. It is estimated that over 300 million mince pies will be eaten over the Christmas period. If you are interested in numbers, maybe 9,875 tonnes of Sprouts will accompany the 10 million Turkeys!!

With these facts and figures in mind, please consider this Bible verse, *"Oh, taste and see that the Lord is good! Blessed is the man who takes refuge in him"* (Psalm 34:8). Christmas is THE time for celebration. It is the greatest anniversary of all time. The fact of Christmas is that God so loved the world, that He sent His own son, Jesus, to be the Saviour of the world. When Jesus was born in Bethlehem, angels descended from heaven and celebrated in song. The fact deserves a feast! Consider another verse from the Psalms, *"Oh, magnify the Lord with me, and let us exalt his name together!"* (Psalm 34:3 ESV)

Image © Dave Bredeson

Nativity

This is the season of traditions, nostalgia, memories and good intentions. Christians celebrate December 25th as the birthday of Jesus, because in 336 AD, the first Christian Roman Emperor, Constantine declared it as the official date. It is the time of the winter solstice, when the sun begins its return orbit around planet earth, and darkness retreats. Thus, it is a fitting analogy for the birthday of Jesus, the Light of the world.

Holly, mistletoe, Christmas trees, carol singing, Father Christmas, presents, feasting on turkey and pudding with a silver sixpence hidden among the currants (until Health and Safety took over!), crackers, and paper hats. All the trimmings of a festive season and then, the first snowdrops, and Christmas is past, again, and sweet spring has come, at last.

However, the most accurate description of Christmas is surely, "Christmas is not just for Christmas day" for the very structure of the universe declares that light always succeeds darkness, day always follows night. The mathematical precision of the orbit of the sun can be calculated for centuries ahead, and Light is infallibly accurate.

May I share my favourite Christmas memory?

I was in charge of the school Nativity play. The choir of angels in white robes, and with paper wings, were mounted on two PE forms, backstage, to be higher up than the rest of the cast. "And remember," I said, "Whatever happens, keep on singing! Angels never stop singing." Came the afternoon of the performance. With energetic exuberance, one of the angels slipped, the PE forms fell, and the angelic host made an undignified descent to the platform. But they kept on singing, they did not miss a note! They righted the forms, climbed back up – and sang! Now, THAT is Christmas.

Whatever happens on planet earth, in political circles, the angels' song is still, *"Peace on earth, goodwill to all men."* Darkness will never overcome the light of the knowledge of the glory of God, in the face of Jesus Christ.

Image © Noel Powell

Nazareth

Jesus the Messiah, great David's greater son, was born in Bethlehem, the city of David, as prophecy foretold. In Hebrew, Bethlehem is known as, "The house of bread," a fitting birthplace for Jesus, who describes Himself as, "The Bread of Life." Carols and cards celebrate this little town, but I want to focus attention on Nazareth, where Jesus grew up.

Nazareth was a small place when Jesus lived there, maybe with a population of less than 400 people. It was a close knit, farming community, traditional and very careful to observe Jewish laws and customs. The language was Aramaic, which is a poetic language: being able to talk well was a valued skill. The Jewish Queen, Salome Alexandra, had long before made reading and writing compulsory for all Jewish boys. To serve the whole of Nazareth, there was just one ancient spring of water. The village seems to have been held in some contempt in First Century Palestine. It is described as a nondescript on the map, with not much to offer! Nearby was the luxurious Greek-style city of Sepphoris, controlled by Herod Antipas. But Nazareth was the place which God chose, with selected parents, for His son, Jesus—truly God and truly man—to grow up and develop His destiny as Saviour of the World! Please consider 7 facts about Nazareth (7 is a perfect number!)

1.   Prophecy said that Messiah would come from Nazareth. "He will be called a Nazarene." God always keeps His word.

2.   Jesus was brought up in an orthodox, God-fearing community. Do you recollect the Proverb, "Train up a child in the right way, and when he is old, he will not depart from it?" God was protecting the humanity of his son.

3.   Jesus is the Word, made flesh. His first language was rich in poetic expression!

4.   The entire population of Nazareth shared water from the same spring. Jesus, the water of life, came to refresh the whole world. There is no other name whereby we can be saved!

5.   In this small community, everyone mattered, and family values were upheld. Consider, then, the words of Jesus, who said that the good shepherd knows his sheep by name.

6. Jesus, the carpenter, possibly worked on some of the exotic buildings in Sepphoris.

7. God's ways are not our ways. In His choice of Nazareth, there is a wisdom which humanity overlooks. Nazareth is famous for one thing, and one thing only. It is the hometown of Jesus!

Image © Digikhmer

The Christmas Tree

The town Christmas tree is truly elegant.! Clear, white lights swirl around the green branches, and beautifully decorate the tree. Christmas trees were introduced to the UK in the Georgian period, when Queen Charlotte and King George 3rd displayed their royal tree at a family Christmas celebration. This royal tradition, emphasised during Queen Victoria's reign, has become a focal point of Christmas for us all. And how appropriate to use a royal tradition to embellish the right royal occasion of Christmas, when the supreme ruler of the Universe, the King of Kings and Lord of Lords, became human for humanity's sake.

The tallest Christmas tree in the UK is a Redwood, planted in Sussex in 1890, and now 33 metres high. Two cranes are used to reach the branches at the top, with 1800 fairy lights making a bright display. This tree really does reach to the stars, but the shape of every Christmas tree, whatever its size, points upward, a reminder of the star of Bethlehem, which shone over the stable when Jesus was born. Astronomers in 21st century now confirm the reality of this star.

The most publicised tree in the UK is the Norwegian spruce, given by the people of Oslo to the people of London every year since 1947. A tree, 20 metres high and maybe 60 years old, is displayed in Trafalgar Square, London, in gratitude that war was ended and there was peace on earth. An evocative gift, since Christmas is the time when we celebrate the birth of Jesus, the Prince of Peace.

On a recent December day, President Trump ordered NASA to start planning a new mission to the Moon, and maybe to Mars! Every December 25th Christians re-identify the possibility of one day traversing the universe and reaching Heaven!

An old carol explains this. "Mild He lays His glory by, Born that man no more may die! Born to raise the sons of earth, Born to give them second birth. Hark, the Herald Angels sing, Glory to the new born King."

Christmas trees are evergreen. This reminds us that God is everlasting, and His love is fresh and bright every new morning.

Your Hairs Are Numbered!

Please consider this sweeping statement recorded as words spoken by Jesus, in Matthews gospel chapter 10. Even the very hairs of your head are all numbered! And now, identify three blessings which are embodied in these words.

First. God knows you intimately. Web search produced this answer to the question, "How many hairs on an average human head?" There are 100,000! Jesus is described as, "the way, THE TRUTH, and the life." (John 14:6) If Jesus declares that God knows and cares for you 100,000 per cent, then that is true.

Secondly, this statement is addressed to YOU. You are just one person amongst 7.5 billion people alive on planet earth. God is concerned with quality before quantity. To Him, you are potential quality, sufficient to ensure you a place in heaven, if you choose to accept His offer of family inclusion, through faith in Jesus Christ. Jesus is THE WAY, he is the only way back to God from the dark paths of sin, he is the light of the world. Re-phrase the verse from Matthew with this emphasis, *"As for you, even the hairs of your head have all been counted"* (Matthew 10:30). 7.5 billion people plus all the people who have lived before and the total is incredible. Yet you can be assured that God is completely concerned about you, He is the Lord God Almighty, the Alpha and the Omega and yet He loves you and me as a father loves his children. He offers us life with Him, through faith in Jesus who is the way, the truth, and THE LIFE.

Thirdly, when children can count to 10, we are pleased. They have yet to learn to understand advanced mathematics. In the same way, God is delighted when we trust Him and obey Him—learn to count to 10, as it were—and He gives us guidance and grace to comprehend the advanced mathematics of the Christian faith through the learning process of life with him here on planet earth. Jesus told his disciples to call God, Father. Jesus explains, *"I assure you that unless you change and become like children, you will never enter the Kingdom of heaven"* (Matthew 18:3). We will not understand the full glory and grace of the godhead until we see Him face to face.

Enjoy the month ahead. Whatever it holds for you, God is in complete control. Jeremiah 29:11 reminds us of this:

"I alone know the plans I have for you, plans to bring you prosperity and not disaster, plans to bring about the future you hope for."

Image © Ig0rzh

Total Eclipse

It is an unchallenged fact that the next total eclipse to be visible in the United Kingdom will occur on September 29th 2090!

It is also a fact that no one refutes the accuracy of this information. Elderly people, whose legs often wobble and let them down on firm flat paths, do not doubt the stability of planet earth, this round ball, spinning at 67,000 miles an hour, in space, without visible means of support. No one has ever fallen off!

Absolute accuracy and precision do not occur by chance. Yet people still doubt the personal presence of God, the Great Designer, Creator, King of Kings, Lord of Lords, and father of Jesus. He gave His only son to live, die and rise from the dead, to be our Saviour and our friend. Because of Jesus, we can know His Father, God, as our Father, in Heaven.

This fact is as unshakable as the fact that you will not fall of the speedily spinning Earth.

I became a Christian over 60 years ago, when I was at College. I am absolutely sure that Jesus who took control of my life then, will be with me until, by death, I exchange time for eternity. As the Salvation Army describe that event – I am anticipating being promoted to glory. My testimony is affirmed by my age, which proves – He saves, He keeps, and He satisfies.

Well now, how about you?